Making the Most of Family Worship

Making the Most of Family Worship

David and Virginia Edens

THE WARNER PRESS

Anderson, Indiana

To
our daughters
Deena and *Debra*
who have helped us make
the most of family worship
and to the thousands of
homes where worship is still
a meaningful experience

CONTENTS

Part I
Worship in the Home

FAMILY WORSHIP

A mammoth motor truck van was parked on the shoulder of a Kentucky highway. The sun let loose the fury of her baking heat. There was no shade where a driver stood idly by the tractor from which a front wheel had been removed. Obviously, he was waiting for help.

A pastor, with a cool car and a warm heart, stopped and offered his assistance. The trucker thanked him, but said he had sent for help. He had burned out a wheel bearing, and another one was on the way. Assured that he could be of no help, the pastor started to pull away.

Then he saw the sign painted in large letters on the side of the van, "Standard Oil Company of Kentucky, Lubricants Division." As the pastor drove off, he exclaimed, "He burned out a bearing—hauling grease!"

God's people can do the same. We can be so engaged in hauling our church cargo, making our rigid schedules, and delivering our religious pay loads that we overlook the essential ingredient—worship—necessary for all our progress. Then we, too, find ourselves burning out bearings.

The Value of Worship

Christians need to understand the spiritual enrichment that worship brings into the life of the believer. William Temple says, "To worship is to quicken the conscience by the holiness of God, to feed the mind with the truth of God, to purge the imagination by the beauty of God, to open the heart to the love of God, to devote the will to the purpose of God."[1]

Worship involves relationship with God, and it is experienced as a person acknowledges the presence of God at any time, in any place.

Albert Orsborn beautifully expresses the desire of one who has worshiped:

> Let the beauty of Jesus be seen in me,
> All His wonderful passion and purity;
> O Thou Spirit divine,
> All my nature refine,
> Till the beauty of Jesus be seen in me.

Personal worship is implemented by eliminating from

our minds all worldly preoccupations and quietly entering God's presence. There our fears, prejudices, tangents, and rebellions will be corrected and balanced by the Holy Spirit.

Worship becomes more meaningful when a special place is made a sanctuary. God said to Moses: "Put off thy shoes from off thy feet, for the place whereon thou standest is holy ground" (Ex. 3:5, KJV). One obvious sanctuary in nature is, perhaps, one of the most overlooked places—your backyard, your own patch of holy ground! In the midst of a busy working day, sanctuary may be in the quietness of a lunch hour listening to music. Housewives and mothers have found spiritual sanctuary even while hands are washing dishes. Relaxation and quietness provide tranquility for thought. On mountains, near the sea, in church, or in a rocking chair, one can be still and know.

George Santayana, who taught so long and brilliantly at Harvard, was born in Spain. His books reveal that he became a master of exquisite English. But he confessed that he was never quite at home in the English tongue. He said: "The roots of the language do not quite reach my center. I never drank in childhood the homely cadences and ditties which in pure, spontaneous poetry set the essential key."

A language never quite reaches the center of our being unless it is learned early and is spoken in the home. This is also true of worship. When it is practiced in the home in the early formative years, it is more meaningful to children than when it is superimposed from outside the home.

Worshiping Together

Family worship offers one of the most significant opportunities for the spiritual development of a Christian, yet it is also one of the most neglected. About nothing related to the Christian family do pastors talk more and parents do less. Consequently, any discussion of family worship is likely to arouse guilt feelings on the one hand and grandiose claims for the practice on the other. In recent years more and more activities take children outside the family setting. The community is absorbing many functions formerly designated as family responsibility. Healthy and wholesome aspects mark much of the social change, but community activities and agencies are no substitute for meaningful family worship experiences.

When members of a family worship together, all their distresses, expectancies, unfoldings, and disciplines are experienced with God. The family gains the strength to meet various situations—the rebelliousness of a child, the unforeseen shock of a serious accident, or death—with a grace and firmness that comes from God. Worshiping together is part of God's plan for Christian families and affords some of their richest experiences.

Husband and wife, parents and children become ministers of God to each other. The gospel must be vigorously communicated within families before it can be effectively expressed to the outside world.

Family worship does not just happen. It is created by conscious effort and design. If your family has not set aside a time for daily worship in the home, now would be a wonderful time to begin. In so doing you would be in the minority (about 6 percent), but you would be in some very good company. Some families have a brief worship time at the close of the morning or evening meal. Perhaps a longer period of worship may be arranged once or twice a week.

The silversmiths of long ago urged the housewives to use their silver every day, for its beauty was enhanced by regular use. What is true of good silver is true of family worship. The experience grows more beautiful and meaningful with use.

Mealtime Devotionals

Samuel M. Shoemaker tells of a college girl who "sat down at a cafeteria table with five other girls, and began by saying grace silently with her head down. The others laughed. When she raised her head she said to them in a nice but firm way: 'What were you laughing at?' They said: 'You know' and went on snickering. 'Aren't you grateful?' she asked. 'For what? We paid for the food,' they said. 'Where did you get the money?' she queried. 'Family,' they said. 'Where did they get the strength— where does it all come from?' she asked. That evening at supper, two more of them said grace. Next day all six of them said it with her." [2]

Saying grace at the table is one way of keeping before the family its desire for God to be supreme in its life. Yet a Gallup poll shows that only four out of every ten families now say grace before meals; whereas, a generation ago the ratio was six out of ten. Another recent survey revealed that in 94 out of every 100 homes no Scripture or devotional reading was done as a family group. Perhaps

Krister Stendahl is right in saying that we live on only 5 percent of our biblical resources.

W. Taliaferro Thompson writes that "a number of graduate students at the University of Chicago, when asked where they got their major ideas in morals and religion, replied, 'Through the conversation in our family at mealtime.'" [3] What a different picture is presented by Anna Laura and Edward W. Gebhard, who quote a college student as saying, "All Dad cares about is making money, and he doesn't care too much how he does it, either. Oh, I know Dad would be shocked to hear me say that. He'd probably like to have me think that what he cares most about is being chairman of the church board of trustees. But you should hear him talk when he sees a chance to make an extra dollar—even at the expense of someone else!" [4]

A fourteen-year-old boy from a broken home heard a blessing asked in a home where he was visiting. He was much impressed. "That was wonderful," he said. "I had the feeling that this family had someone bigger and stronger than themselves to call on." That feeling, developed in a Christian family, may hold through life.

Anyone who has tried to have family worship knows that it is not easy and that the pattern of yesterday cannot necessarily be preserved. It is so hard to get the family together that in some homes meals are served cafeteria style. The whole group rarely sits down at once. Even when they are together, they are so pressed for time that it is difficult to set aside a few, worshipful quiet moments from the feverish hurry of their lives. If father is there, he has to get to work on time. The children have to leave for school on different schedules. If mother works, she is rushed too. Even if several minutes are salvaged, creating a spiritual atmosphere is difficult in a family whose life is immersed in secular culture. To have meaningful family worship day after day requires careful planning.

Most families can pause for grace before meals. The table is a symbol of family unity; there are "many beds, but one board." If more time were allowed for grace before the meal and for unhurried conversation during it, when even the youngest child could say what was on his mind, life in the home might be transformed.

In thanking God for our daily bread we do more than affirm our good fortune in material blessings. We recognize the presence of Christ as the unseen guest in our homes. Grace at mealtime is a profound symbol of our place in the family of God. In the Bible, bread is recognized as being more than food. It is also evidence of God's grace. It is an integral part of the Lord's Supper which symbolizes Christ's life, death, burial, and resurrection. This symbol of man's redemption did not happen just by chance. The broken bread and poured wine also are symbols of our physical needs for bread and drink. We are dependent upon the mercy of God for food.

Like the ancient Hebrew family, we too should pray: "Blessed art thou, O Lord our God, who bringest forth bread from the ground." The Hebrew home has been deeply religious since Old Testament times.

Sharing a sabbath meal in the home of Rabbi David Jacobson was one of the most meaningful family and religious experiences my wife and I have had. The family gathers around the festive sabbath table. First the mother lights the candles and officially welcomes the sabbath queen, or bride, with a prayer. The glow of the candles is reflected in her eyes as members of the family are gathered together. The sabbath is a family time and also a time of thanksgiving. The father lifts the cup of wine and recites the *kiddush* or sanctification blessing. The family is grateful for all the good things which have come into their lives since the last sabbath. As they recite the *matzo* prayer over bread, each member shows his appreciation for the privilege of enjoying the bounty of God's world. Then the father takes a piece of sabbath *hallah* bread and shares it with each member of the family. As God is one, so is the Jewish family at sabbath time.

After dinner the family brings the sabbath queen, or bride, as its guest to the temple. Again the candles are lit and the *kiddush* is recited. The family prays and thanks God for all the days of the week—the days of work and study, the days of joy, this special (sabbath) day—and for family and worship time. When the service ends, everyone wishes each other *Gut shabbos*, "A good sabbath." In many congregations a greeting of *Shabbat shalom u-vrachah*, "Sabbath peace and blessings," is used. Very often, an informal program which includes the serving of refreshments will follow the service. This gathering is known as an *Oneg shabbat*, or the "Joy of the sabbath."

The strength of the Jews, despite centuries of persecution, is largely attributable to the spiritual unity of their family life.

Grace at meals may be expressed in many and varied ways. Some families pray a memorized grace together.

Others sing a hymn. Some repeat a verse of Scripture. Some pray the well-loved prayer that Jesus taught in response to his disciple's request, "Lord, teach us to pray." Those prayers are best which are an expression of each individual in the family.

Mealtime is an easy and natural occasion for worship in the home. Motivated by love of God and fellowman, prayers of gratitude further bind the members together. If the routine seems empty, motivation and method may require change. Gratitude to God before meals is not on trial; the workability of faith in Christ may be.

Out-of-door Worship

Family camping, vacation trips, and picnics are part of the American way of life. These outings afford unique opportunities for meaningful family worship. Jesus said, "Come ye yourselves apart into a desert place, and rest a while: for there were many coming and going, and they had no leisure so much as to eat" (Mark 6:31, KJV). This describes our situation—hurrying in crowds, racing with the clock, living "the breathless life."

No leisure for eating is a small loss compared to no leisure for living in the deepest sense, no leisure for the spirit to expand. The great spiritual and psychological risk of such a life is that a person may fail to find his true self. We need to discriminate as to what really feeds our inner needs of taste and enjoyment. We are to be masters and not slaves of the material life. The attainment of this relationship to things requires the development of spiritual appreciation and commitment.

How we spend our leisure is related to the ultimate

concern of life itself; it runs throughout the search for meaning. The problems of fear, anxiety, or boredom may be related to the family's alienation from God and fellow-man. The depth of this alienation shows in the use which the family makes of its unstructured hours. Here, despair and lack of creativity show first and in greatest depth.

God's creation is good and is to be enjoyed. Yet with all the variety and choice of leisure activities, the few people who seem to enjoy themselves these days is amazing. Maybe this is because we have missed Jesus' injunction to "seek first his kingdom and his righteousness, and all these things shall be yours as well" (Matt. 6:33).

So the words of Jesus, "Come ye yourselves apart into a desert place and rest awhile," are a helpful guide—rest in a quiet place to regain depleted physical and mental strength. And it should be done in a way best suited to our needs. If we are too busy to rest, then we are too busy. After we have caught our emotional breath, we can return to the crowds without being spiritually crushed by them.

The out-of-doors provides a natural setting for communing with God and for learning respect and reverence for his creation. These lovely nature Scripture passages can add strength, beauty, and meaning when the family worships together out-of-doors: Psalms 8:3-9; 19; 65:9-13; 95:1-6; 104:1-24; 147; 148:1-13, and Genesis 1; 2:1-3.

Certain hymns become more significant when sung out-of-doors by the family:

> Day Is Dying in the West
> Now the Day Is Over

God Who Touchest Earth with Beauty
This Is My Father's World

Two paper-bound books offer helpful suggestions for enhancing worship services in the out-of-doors: Barbara Peck Poppe's *Let's Find Outdoor Opportunities for Worship,* for parents with children ages one to six, and Mary Elizabeth Mason's *Let the Bible Speak Out of Doors,* for parents with children ages six to twelve.

Various church denominations have developed and published materials suited for family worship. Some of these are listed at the end of this book.

How can we get family worship started? What can parents do to make family worship more meaningful for many different ages and situations? The following chapters may prove helpful.

WITH YOUNG CHILDREN

Having young children in our homes is a blessing to treasure. All too soon the years slip away, and these little ones grow up and leave. We do not want to waste one precious moment spent with them.

Part of our joy in these young ones is the privilege of leading them to God through Jesus Christ. To be able to show a child God's love is a thrilling experience. Children respond to the beauty of God revealed in the world. They can respond to his holiness, and their eager minds can reach for the truth of God. They can know his love.

Devotions with young children are not always a quiet, serene time. More than once we have had to retrieve the youngest member of our family from under the table. Heads bowed devotedly have often freed little hands to do some mischief. The attention span of young children, particularly the preschooler, is very short. They tire when family worship lasts more than a few minutes. The sincere, confident, loving approach to God reveals parental faith long before the spoken word can be fully understood.

Appropriate time for family worship with young children varies. Vivid moments of worship and wonder may occur as God's creation is revealed through a sudden shower, a rainbow, a sunset, the song of a cardinal, or while looking at a snowflake through a magnifying glass. Worship may occur as an expression of gratitude to God for freshly baked bread. It could happen spontaneously during a happy family celebration. Worship may be planned when a new baby is welcomed home, or a birthday is celebrated. It may be at the beginning of the day, at mealtime, or as the child is ready for bed. For worship to be a part of ordinary events of life is important. Sometimes, we worship when everything goes dead wrong, or when our hearts are heavy with sadness—whenever experiences lead us into God's presence.

How shall we interpret God to young children?

Jesus taught that God is a Father who is loving, considerate, and sympathetic. God's fatherhood embodies all that is best in earthly parents plus a deeper, all-inclusive love, unexplainable to children but which they sense as they live with adults who exemplify a wise and understanding love.

God the Creator is the giver of good and perfect gifts. Jesus taught that our relationship is one of father and children and that prayers are addressed to him as Father: "When you pray, say, 'Father.'"

But we must safeguard young children from an interpretation of God as a glorified Santa Claus. He does not "send rain" and "send sunshine" just to suit our wishes. God's wonderful plan for the cycle of seasons, for rain, and for sunshine is beyond our understanding. Your child's church school materials may help you to interpret God to your children. Often they contain suggestions you can use as you plan your worship.

Prayer before meals has been practiced for generations. A family can begin this practice by thanking God for his blessings and for food set before them. Help your children to participate by asking them to give a sentence prayer, or to tell what they are thankful for. Here is a simply expressed prayer that can be used by the family which is just beginning this custom in their home:

> God is great, God is good,
> And we thank him for this food;
> By his hand may all be fed,
> Give us, Lord, our daily bread.

A very meaningful prayer is:

> O God, we thank Thee—
> For life through food,

> For happiness through friends,
> For fellowship through love, and
> For eternal life through Jesus Christ.

A rural family which knows the process of producing bread from the earth might use the following verse:

> Back of the loaf is the snowy flour,
> And back of the flour the mill,
> And back of the mill is the wheat and the shower,
> And the sun and the Father's will.

This prayer will appeal to a very young child:

> For all these glad hours
> Of work and play,
> For food and rest
> At close of day,
> We thank thee,
> Heavenly Father.

Another meaningful prayer for a young child is:

> Thank you for the world so sweet,
> Thank you for the food we eat,
> Thank you for the birds that sing,
> Thank you, God, for everything.
> —E. H. Leatham

More important to children than the words we use to express our gratitude to God are the manner and attitude in which the words are spoken. Although children can participate and take turns in bringing a meaningful worship experience to the family, parents should direct the worship. Parents, and grandparents too, add to the richness of the experience with their greater facility of expression.

At times, families will enjoy "singing graces." Some are simple enough to be sung well by every member. Widely used is "Be Present at Our Table Lord," sung to the tune of Old Hundredth.

The "Quaker Grace" is used in some families with young children. Around the table, with hands joined and heads bowed, each person has a moment of silent prayer in grateful appreciation for God's good gifts. This can be effectively done when the family eats together in a public place. Never underestimate the impression of a reverent attitude, which a bowed head creates, on the mind of a young child.

Let the children sing a song they have learned and then have the family sing it together. Lois Vogel's *God and Your Family* (Concordia Publishing House, 1963) is a devotional book written especially for families with children ages four through nine.

To make Bible stories come to life for young children use three-dimensional and other kinds of drama scenes. These will help them to visualize the stories as they are read or told. Check your publishing house catalogues or religious bookstores for packets of these kinds of materials.

Children can be encouraged to make their own illustrations by finger painting, paper tearing, drawings, and cutouts. As they get involved in the action they will get the story message more clearly. They may want to dramatize the stories themselves. Puppets may be used to tell the stories. These can be made quite simply. Children love this method of storytelling.

> Happy the home where prayer is heard,
> And praise is wont to rise;
> Where parents love the sacred Word
> And all its wisdom prize.
>
> —Henry Ware

WITH MIXED AGES

In a letter to Philemon, Paul sent greetings also to Apphia, his wife, to Archippus—evidently their son—and "to the church that is in thy house." Similar references are found in Romans 16:5, 1 Corinthians 16:19, and Colossians 4:15. These little groups of "called-out ones" met in homes, even as people frequently do on mission fields today.

The Scriptures seem to suggest that the church and the home have been closely related from the beginning, that the Christian home is a church and the Christian church is a family. Each performs distinctive functions, but they also share some in common.

Just as the pastor of a church has difficulty gearing his sermon to reach all ages, so does the leader of family worship have some problems where his "audience" is one of widely separated ages and interests. An effort was made in one congregation to discover how some of its families were conducting their worship. In one, there were five children ranging in age from three to fourteen; in another, six children with a fourteen-year age spread; in others, only two or three children, not far apart in age, or just one child. What would be ideal for one family obviously would not suit another. Parents need to be particularly attentive to keeping a balance of participation between older children and younger ones and allow neither to dominate the time day after day.

As the family grows in appreciation of worship together, it may want to follow the custom shared here by a family of five:

Each Monday evening every member of the family comes to the dinner table with something special to share with the entire group. Sometimes it is a choice verse of Scripture, sometimes a bit of poetry composed by the one who shares it, it may be a short story, a true experience out of the week's activities, a song, and even a drawing or a clay-sculptured horse; once it was the first jonquil from the garden, another time a basket of freshly-made rolls. The main course for these evening meals is always a casserole dish so that the dinner may stay hot for serving immediately following the sharing of the treasures. The family speaks in glowing terms of the good conversation which accompanies the meal on these Monday evening occasions. The children look forward to their part in the sharing experience.[5]

In our family we have practiced this. "The Five Senses," written by one of our daughters when she was nine, is a special sharing:

> I open my eyes,
> And what do I see?
> The grass, trees, flowers,
> And one buzzing bee.
>
> I listen with my ears,
> And what do I hear?
> A tiny baby crying,
> And shedding a tear.
>
> I breathe through my nose,
> And what do I smell?
> A flower so sweet,
> And made quite well.
>
> I touch with my hands,
> And what do I feel?
> A furry pussy-willow,
>   some grain,
> And a rose so real.
>
> I open my mouth,
> And what do I say?
> Thank you, O God,
> For night and for day.

Religious book stores have recordings for different age groups which may be used to supplement family worship.

Some religious bookstores and publishing houses carry albums of children's songs which would be most helpful aids for family worship. Some of these are available at various age levels. Check catalogues.

Louis Evans' recording, *Love, Marriage and God,* presents short talks on the secret of a happy marriage and a happy home. This forms a good basis for discussing preparation for Christian marriage with the older children. There is no better atmosphere for such a discussion than during the time of family worship.

Many passages in the Bible speak with refreshing boldness and frankness on the subject of marriage: Ephesians 5:18 to 6:4; 1 Peter 3:1-8; 1 Corinthians 7:3-5; 1 Corinthians 13. Read them from a modern translation such as J. B. Phillips' *The New Testament in Modern English.* These passages giving Christian interpretations of marriage and sex can lead to a discussion of sex which places it in proper perspective. Sidonie M. Gruenberg's *The Wonderful Story of How You Were Born* provides good material for discussing the birth process.

Many children enjoy discussing great religious paintings. You may want to make a collection of some. Using a book, such as Cynthia Maus's *Christ and the Fine Arts,* let each member of the family say how well he thinks the artist has represented the Bible story.

Children have a remarkable readiness for reverence. A parent, who is constantly on the alert to the normal questions that children ask at different ages, will discover a growing awareness of God. A young child's praying is normally self-centered. Gradually he develops a concern for others, and his prayer thoughts deepen. This comes with consistent experience. It is learned by imitation of adults or older children whose spoken prayers recall the needs of the world's people, offer thanksgiving for life's gifts, or make petitions in accord with God's will.

WITH OLDER CHILDREN

"Addle-essence" is a most trying time in a "tween-agers" life, because he then balances precariously between childhood and physiological maturity. As a result, the adolescent demonstrates extreme contrasts at times—all for or all against. On other occasions, he wears a mask of utter indifference. During this time, the older child is usually filled with doubts and questions about his faith and his place in the universe. This is a normal, healthy sign of growth. A parent's task is to direct his interest to a cause that he will pursue. But, no matter how lofty the project, he is capable of shrugging it off if his interest is not willingly captured.

Youthful Christian character is nurtured not in the fleeting moments of glorious experience but in the common activities of everyday affairs, in a continuous, often undramatic, commitment. What counts is the consistent family training and experience over the years, not the few high points or the blundering and jarring mistakes. Daily family worship may seem prosaic at times, but it produces good results in the long run.

Family worship builds a common loyalty to God and to one another if the presence of the Holy Spirit is really allowed expression through the thoughts and actions of family members in the home. Properly directed, young people can find in God's Word guidance for life and meaning for existence—God loves, and seeks, and saves. The history of that process is best described in the Scriptures.

The teen-ager may feel that he has outgrown family worship, but he is in a period of growth when he needs it most. The more normal and natural the participation by the children, the better. All should actively participate, but the father should direct the worship period. Family worship will mean more to growing children, particularly to the sons in the home, if the father dignifies this worship by taking the lead.

The older children may be asked to read the Scripture, to lead in prayer, or occasionally to conduct the entire worship service. Older boys and girls take pride in reading from their own Bibles. Provide each child with *Good News for Modern Man: The New Testament in Today's*

English, an excellent and very inexpensive translation by the American Bible Society. The children may take turns reading from "The Family Worships" section of *Home Life* magazine, or from other devotional materials.

Helpful books in this area are Charles S. Mueller's God's *Wonderful World of Words: Devotions for Families with Children Ages 9-13* and J. Herbert Gilmore's *Devotions for the Home.* Materials should always be adapted to the particular needs of the family.

An older child may do a special study in some area of the Christian life and report his findings to the family.

Hymns often have special meaning for older children. Their world is expanding and their interests are increasing. Utilize their talents in music if they play an instrument or sing. A hymn of special significance for older children is: "This Is My Father's World."

Another hymn, "For the Beauty of the Earth," emphasizes "the wonder of each hour," "the joy of human love," "Thy church evermore." The older child is experiencing these things in his family and his world.

Music is of great importance in influencing the lives of people. Andrew Fletcher, the Scottish politician, is credited with saying, "Let me make the songs of a nation, and I care not who makes its laws." Who can measure the influence of music in the home? The simplest lullaby seems to have a mystical power to calm an infant. A hymn, planted in the receptive mind of a child, can awaken aspirations that will carry a life-long impact.

A lad, facing the merciless fire of a machine gun in a blazing battle during World War II, tells how he was sustained by remembering the words of "Abide with

Me" which his mother sang while she performed the menial chores of the home.

It is good to sing our gratitude as well as to speak it. The message of a single stanza or refrain of a song often lingers in the minds of children long after a prayer has been forgotten. A simple prayer song, such as "Have Thine Own Way, Lord" or "Into My Heart," can unite the family in a spirit of prayer and devotion.

WITH NO CHILDREN

One purpose for the establishment of the home is to rear children and, later, to send them as mature persons into the world. To have been a good mother or father is a real accomplishment. More than ever, the American family needs to incorporate into its life the values of the Christian faith.

The couple who keeps faith with God will remain strong. Worshiping together, believing, trusting, and praying creates a unity that cannot be broken. Can you name a couple who went to the divorce court who prayed *to-*

gether the week before they went? Relationship to God through Christ builds sound character for any crisis.

Many couples omit family worship after the children leave home or when there are no children. In retirement, some wives find they have half as much pay and twice as much husband. Both can create problems. In daily family worship, common problems can be discussed and prayed about together.

Communication is necessary if a couple is to live together meaningfully—better an argument than silent hostility. Biblically, husbands and wives are admonished to have adequate communication: "Likewise you husbands, live considerately with your wives, bestowing honor on the woman as the weaker sex, since you are joint heirs of the grace of life, in order that your prayers may not be hindered" (1 Peter 3:7). On the husband is placed the burden of responsibility in the husband-wife relationship. He is specifically instructed to live with her considerately.

The husband is to live his life in such a way that he can be with his wife. Work and other preoccupations which cause him to be away from her too much should be resisted. When he does have to be away from her, he must remember that she is a joint heir of the grace of life with him and must be taken into consideration in his planning. This is especially true when there are no children in the home.

C. S. Anderson Scott tells us that there are three dimensions to love: *attention, consideration,* and *care.* The husband attends to his wife's needs and does not rely on other people in the community to do for her what only he can do—be an attentive husband, listening to his wife's concerns and problems and profiting from her revelation of herself to him as a person.

There is no substitute for spiritual relationships within the home. Sometimes illness causes marital partners to become aware of neglect. A medical doctor said to the husband of a patient: "If you will spend a little time every day with your wife attending to her concerns, you won't have to spend so much all at once!"

Love is characterized by considerateness. This means that husbands are to heed what wives say and do. They are to be regarded as needing protection, friendship, and guidance. In times of fulfilling their responsibility of bearing children, they are indeed rather helpless.

But being the weaker sex does not mean that woman is inferior. To the contrary, she is a joint heir in the redemption which Jesus Christ has brought. The considerate husband does not place his responsibilities on the shoulders of his wife, but he carries them himself even as he also considers her needs.

Love is characterized by care. The husband not only gives attention and considerateness to his wife, he demonstrates to her that he cares what happens to her. He cares for her in sickness and health. He cares for her way of doing things. He is committed unconditionally to her. He carries through with his promises to her.

Love of such threefold quality transforms Christian marriage. Communication with each other again and again overflows into communion with God. This communion may burst forth like a sunrise. It may recede like a sunset.

The Scriptures also say that, without the considerateness and joint inheritance of the grace of life, the prayers of husband and wife may be thwarted. Failure of communication occurs when husband and wife have little or no time together. Misunderstandings grow out of communication failures. Conflict increases. Loss of confidence ensues. Suspicion and disrespect emerge. The couple is in trouble. Prayer becomes a perfunctory formality and not a fellowship of husband and wife. Eventually, communion with God ceases.

Sometimes a husband and wife become idolaters of each other. Expecting each other to be perfect, each loses patience when the other one is not. Little or no forgiveness is forthcoming. Carelessness, harshness, and neglect take the place of carefulness, considerateness, and attentiveness. And only the desperation of "What on earth are we going to do?" remains. But at this point, the Scriptures help again: "Do not cheat each other of normal sexual intercourse, unless of course you both decide to abstain temporarily to make special opportunity for fasting and prayer. But afterward you should resume relations as before, or you will expose yourselves to the obvious temptation of the devil" (1 Cor. 7:5, Phillips).[6]

The failure of a couple with no children to communicate and to have intimate relationships may obstruct each individual's relationship to God in prayer. By their individual prayers a couple nourishes and sustains their prayers together. Misunderstandings that arise in marriage are fewer, and the joys of harmonious oneness in Christ are multiplied.

BEGINNING FAMILY WORSHIP

An old cookbook begins a recipe for preparing rabbit stew with a statement: "First catch the rabbit." The first step in establishing family worship in the home is the decision to do it. Take into consideration particular family problems and select the best time for all concerned. Sensitive parents see opportunities for worship in everyday experiences and special occasions. Nevertheless, there must be a time, a place, and a pattern. These externals are necessary for family worship—just as they are for church worship. Without them, family worship is not likely to be a reality.

Some may argue that family worship together at a set time is contrived and will result in an artificial performance rather than a genuine worship experience. The danger is that without a definite time, members of a family may have grown so spiritually insensitive that they fail to recognize a worship opportunity when it comes.

The prayer life of the home must be intentionally planned.

It will take purpose to bring about the establishment of Christian living in the homes of America. The materials, the literature, the techniques necessary for religious life in the home are available. What is lacking is the will to use them, the will to be spiritual parents, the will to acknowledge openly and gladly our love of God to one another within the family. All of this awaits the intentional commitment of each one of us to a definite plan that includes the worship of God daily in the home. We need to plan as definitely the time and the way for meeting this great need in our lives as we plan for meals, recreation, and rest.[7]

The devotional leader, child or parent, should read through the devotional material beforehand and have his Bible properly opened to the suggested text. He should practice reading the devotion until its meaning is clearly understood. The leader may wish to apply the devotional to an incident in family life. Strive for variety. Monotony and dull forms soon defeat good Christian intent.

Whether the children are young or old, many or few, or none at all, goals should be realistic. Each member of the family probably will not have a genuine experience of worship each time family worship is conducted. But if even one member learns some new truth, gains fresh insight, or finds strength for some trial or temptation that day, the family is blessed.

> So long as there are homes where fires burn
> And there is bread,
> So long as there are homes where lamps are lit
> And prayers are said;
> Although a people falters through the dark
> And nations grope,
> With God himself back of these little homes
> We still can hope.[8]

The following fifty devotionals are centered around great themes of the Bible. It is our hope that they will be helpful in making family worship more meaningful for all who use them.

Part II Fifty Devotionals

THE FAMILY'S COMMUNION WITH GOD

Unto Your Children
(Read Luke 11:5–13)

Earthly fathers are expected to provide what is best for their children on the basis of what will be most beneficial for their sons and daughters in all areas of their lives.

A parent sees that a child takes immunization shots. The child may not understand the reason for this moment of hurt, but the parent knows the vital protection that vaccines provide against disease. While parents encourage increasing independence in some areas of a teen-ager's experience, they must set definite limitations in other areas because they know the reasons for certain restraints and self-discipline being necessary.

When communication between parents and children is open and free, sons and daughters confidently ask for parental judgment and decision. Wise and sensitive parents cannot give their children everything they ask for, but they are usually eager to give themselves in love. This is even more true of our Heavenly Father.

God may not give us all the things we ask for, but Jesus has assured us that God is always ready to give his best gift—the Holy Spirit. However, this gift becomes ours only after we ask for it. A father can provide the *things* his children need before they ask for them. But a father cannot give his *love* until the child is ready to receive it.

Petitionary prayer is an act of exploration by which we discover God's will.

(Read again verse 10 in the Scripture passage and close the worship time with sentence prayers.)

And Pray Always
(Read Luke 21:10–19, 34–36)

The pressures of the competitive business world, the daily monotony of housework, or even retirement can crush our souls unless we learn to hear what Thoreau calls "a different drummer." God meant for us to be more than faceless, conforming status-seekers in a world grasping for money.

We do not live just to die and be buried, like Willy in *Death of a Salesman,* never really knowing anything about ourselves. But we cannot find self-identification or sustain our integrity apart from the God who made us.

The secret of Jesus' sustained life and power was the continual opening of his soul in prayer to God. For us, also, this is the secret of the sustained life of the spirit. There can be little spiritual self-fulfilment without the solitude of prayer. Without it, life lacks the height of inspiration, the depth of steadfastness, and the breadth of understanding.

For many people, their living conditions make a place of solitude impossible. A young woman picturesquely described the situation to her pastor: "You tell us that Jesus said to enter your closet and close the door. In our apartment there are no closets, and there are no doors." Much of life has become public. It is hard to shut our doors against the insistent intrusions of the outer world, of radio and television, and other constant invaders of the solitary place.

However, we must find a place for private prayer. We must do it where we can. And always, God is still to be found in the inner sanctuary of our souls.

Our Father, help us to pray always that we may stand before Thee redeemed and mature. We pray in the name of thy son. Amen.

Strength and Comfort
(Read John 14:15–21)

An American girl received a beautiful letter from her fiancé, a soldier in the Korean War. In strong, brave words he wrote of his love for her, of his faith in God, and of the Comforter's presence in his life. If his life were spared, he wanted it to count in the work of God's Kingdom. The young man also revealed his willingness to die if that were required.

The young woman read the letter to her best friend. A few days later, she received the sad news of her soldier-sweetheart's death. The letter became inexpressibly dear and sacred to this young woman. Her best friend, with whom she had shared her fiancé's letter, asked if she might read it to her Sunday School class because it bore such a significant witness.

At first, the young girl refused the request. She felt that his last words were not for others, that this love letter was meant only for her. Then gradually she realized the selfishness of her grief; she must let this soldier do his work for the kingdom through his written words. As the letter was shared with others, it became instrumental in leading many people to know the Lord whom the soldier loved.

Something like this happens when Jesus' words are read. Just before he was betrayed and crucified, he spoke many beautiful, tender words to his disciples. Afterwards, they found strength and comfort in recalling the Saviour's farewell words.

Happily for us and for all the world, John recorded these promises in his Gospel. They have provided strength and consolation to countless followers from that day to this. The Bible is God's love letter to every member of our family.

(Let members of the family tell of times when they have been strengthened and comforted by God's promises.)

We thank thee, our Father, in Jesus' name for the comfort we feel because of thy love for us. Amen.

Hold My Hand
(Read Hebrews 4:14 to 5–5)

Seven-year-old Debra fell on a rock and cut her eyelid. Her mother knew that the help of a doctor was necessary. When they reached the doctor's office, he said that a few stitches were needed. The surgeon gently told Debra that he would have to stick her with a needle. He asked if she could sit very still without jumping.

Quite simply the little girl answered: "I can, if Mother will hold my hand." The mother lifted Debra to her lap, steadied her against her shoulder, slipped her arms around the little girl's waist and held her two small hands. The doctor took the necessary stitches, and Debra did not flinch.

What good did holding Mother's hand do? Not one less stitch was taken. No less pain was endured. Mother's arms had provided the comfort needed for this little girl to accept what had to be done.

God's grace is like that. Knowing his love, we can say, "Yes, I can endure this if God will hold my hand." This is indeed a most realistic comfort to the Christian in time of need. God is always available when we go to him through Christ.

Dear Lord, may we come boldly to thee for help. We thank thee for thy love and mercy. Help us to demonstrate this in our family. This we ask in the name of Jesus Christ our Lord. Amen.

Acts Are for Doing
(Read Psalm 107:1-9)

The acrostic below might be printed on a chalkboard or poster.

A doration
C onfession
T hanksgiving
S upplication

Worship consists of *acts* in which we participate—*adoration* for God, *confession* of sins, *thanksgiving* for

God's goodness and wonderful works, and *supplication* and concern for others.

The Scripture passage today emphasizes adoration and thanksgiving.

Over 550 times the Bible uses the word "praise" or "rejoice." Praise of God is associated with our thanksgiving to him and should be a natural part of Christian living and worship. We in America have so much to be thankful for—freedom of speech, our schools and churches, our homes, and freedom to worship. But too often we fail to express our thanks and praise to God for these gifts. An unthankful man is like a hog under a tree eating acorns and never looking up to see where they came from. Everyone can be thankful for something. "I complained because I had no shoes, until I met a man who had no feet."

(Ask each member of the family to tell what he is especially thankful for today. Join hands as one member prays.)

Dear God, accept the gratitude of our hearts this day, and make us ever mindful of the source of every good and perfect gift. We pray in Jesus name. Amen.

An Everlasting Covenant
(Read Genesis 17:1–8)

This passage is not a two-way conversation between God and Abraham. God is talking; but as he talks, a relationship of holy familiarity between the Mighty God and his servant is revealed. Notice how many times God said, "I will." He reveals his power again and again to Abraham.

Abraham is the only person in the Old Testament referred to as "the friend of God" (James 2:23). When he was ninety-nine years old, the Lord promised Abraham a new blessing with the birth of Isaac.

Along with the new blessings, there were to come also new responsibilities for Abraham. God called upon him to live and move in the divine presence: "Walk before me, and be thou perfect."

Sunday School teachers often ask a group of young children, "Who are your friends?" One answer usually given is, "God is our friend." A parent asks a young child, "What does God mean to you?" Simply and positively the child replies "Why, he's my best friend." We can talk with God as we would with a good friend next door—in a relationship of trust. Sometimes there are barriers that limit a meaningful communication between us and God. These same barriers can limit the development of meaningful earthly friendships.

God's rich blessings and promises require from us responsibility and commitment. Enjoying friendship with God means walking with him every day. God always has some fresh surprise for a Christian as he grows and matures in spiritual experience and in fellowship with God.

(The meaning of friendship might be discussed here. In each age and stage of life we need friends. Teen-agers will have different ideas from those of the preschool child.)

Heavenly Father, make us worthy, through Jesus Christ, of thy friendship. Amen.

A God of Grace and Mercy
(Read Psalm 116:1–9 and sing or read together "Amazing Grace.")

These verses speak of grace. What does grace mean? We may think of social grace—the kind, thoughtful ways that people have. Or we may think of grace which we say before meals—the prayer of thankfulness. If we had borrowed money from a bank and later found that we were unable to return the payment within a stated time, the bank probably would give fifteen days grace. The bank likely would charge interest during the fifteen days grace. If a borrower fails to pay back the loan, the bank may take his car, claim his furniture, or other possessions.

God's grace is unlike a bank's grace—or any other kind of repayment which men require. God frees us from the debt and penalty of our sins and requires no further payment from us because Jesus paid the entire debt for

us. We experience that "amazing grace" the moment we
believe in Christ and accept him as our Saviour.

(Close with sentence prayers from family members, ex-
pressing gratitude to God for his goodness and mercy.)

He Maketh the Storm a Calm
(Read Psalm 107:23–32)

Does God really answer prayer? If he does, how?
Through the ages, prayer has had its critics. Some say,
"I do not believe in prayer." Yet, for every one person who
is skeptical, there are hundreds who live with no shadow
of doubt. They know that prayer is communication with
a living God because he has demonstrated that he has
heard their prayers.

Like the psalmist, we all have cried unto the Lord in
our trouble, and he has brought us out of distress. He has
calmed our storms.

If prayer is not answered, this truth would have been
discovered by some noble and intelligent men of integrity,
and prayer would have been renounced a long time ago.
The spiritual world, which has been experienced by men
across the centuries, is not a baseless product of man's
imagination. It is a real world, as real as the world in
which we see, touch, hear, smell, and taste. Prayer is just
as real as love and beauty.

*Regard, O Lord, with thy Fatherly compassion, all who
are disquieted and troubled, who cannot lose themselves
either in happy work by day or in restful sleep by night.
Lead us, we pray thee, out of the storm into quietude, out
of futility into usefulness, out of despair into the sure
serenity of thy truth. Amen.*

In God We Trust
(Read 2 Kings 17:7–18)

Many people in our nation are distracted by a
variety of things which separate them from God who is
the very center of life. The devil is a specialist in getting
people to major on minors, to serve idols.

Israel sinned by serving the idols which men created
rather than the true and living God who revealed himself.

(Discuss some things that indicate to the world that
our nation recognizes and is dependent upon God: chap-
lains in the armed forces; prayer before Congress meets;
prayer at national conventions; "In God We Trust" on
our money; "under God" in our pledge; the President's
taking oath of office with his hand laid upon the Bible.
Is there a danger that these observances can become
mere routine and thereby lose their vitality?

Have the family members look at the hymn "My

Country, 'Tis of Thee," written by a Baptist clergyman, Samuel F. Smith. Ask a member to read the first verse. Note each phrase and ask what is meant by them. Have another member read the last verse as the closing prayer.)

THE FAMILY'S RELATION
TO THE CHURCH

You Are the Christ
(Read Matthew 16:13–19)

In the play *The Green Pastures* one of the characters says: "Everything nailed down is coming loose."

Often, we feel that this is true in times of personal, family, and world crises. There are new frontiers in space, and we have lost our sense of security. When the winds of strife, turmoil, and violence sweep our world it certainly does seem that "everything nailed down is coming loose."

(The person leading the family worship may ask: "Do you think this statement is true?" Let each one comment.)

Our fears and doubts pull out the nails of security, and the once orderly structure of life becomes like so many loose boards hurled through the sky by hurricane winds. Many people find themselves at loose ends morally and intellectually.

But in the midst of all of this disorder, turmoil, and insecurity some things remain. The winds of change, revolution, and rebellion are powerless to destroy the truth that Peter declared: "You are the Christ, the Son of the living God."

This affirmation is the foundation of the Christian church. Jesus blessed Peter for his belief. He will bless our family as we affirm our loyalty and commitment to him. There are many ways of confessing Christ today. We can go before the church and state that we have accepted him. We can train for places of service. Most of all, we can practice his presence in our family circle in such ways that others may see him in us.

Dear Heavenly Father, we want to confess in every way possible that Jesus is the Christ, the Son of the living God. Make his presence a reality in our home and church. In his name we pray. Amen.

The Church United
(Read 1 Corinthians 12:4–13)

Once upon a summertime, the bedraggled congregation of a small church was singing the second stanza of "Onward, Christian Soldiers." As they dragged out the words, "Onward, then, ye people, join our happy throng," three things seemed to be wrong with their effort: they were no throng, they obviously were not happy, and they didn't appear to care whether anyone joined them or not. Three strikes and out!

It is sad when such an atmosphere prevails in a church, a home, or a Sunday School class. Genuine fellowship is not optional for Christian growth; it is imperative! The community of faith—the church—can be shattered by the callous indifference which exalts secondary issues but ignores the central obligations of love and fellowship.

A young man who committed suicide left a note saying: "My life is a mistake. I never should have been born. I want to ask the world one question: What's the purpose in living?" If this young man had been welcomed to some cordial, Christian fellowship and had been made to feel that he was a part of it, he likely would never have felt so desolate as to have committed suicide.

(Talk about what Christian fellowship offers that is not found elsewhere. Ask family members to think of individuals who lack the security of the Christian fellowship to be found in a church. Suggest ways of surrounding these persons with love and concern that would express to them the joy of belonging to such a fellowship. Close

with a prayer asking God to lead each one present to be a
faithful member of the body of Christ. Pray especially
for any unchurched person named by family.)

Who's Boss?
(Read Colossians 1:9–20)

A family was discussing verse 18 of this Scripture passage as they rode home from church one Sunday
when the youngest child commented: "I thought Brother
Jones was the boss of the church, like you are the boss at
home, Daddy."

Like the Colossians, this boy did not understand
Christ's leaderhip in the church. Paul declared that the
nature, power, and purpose of God are fully imparted to
the world through Jesus' redemptive life on earth and his
resurrection; he is, thereby, head and Lord of the church.

The church is the body of Christ. In the human body,
the afferent nerves communicate to the brain (head) the
sensations of each organ. The efferent nerves convey im-
pulses from the brain (head) that control the movements
of the body. In the church, as the body of Christ, he, as
its head, is conscious of the experiences of every member.
He directs and guides the action of every member, unless
the person is paralyzed by the sin of his own wilfulness.
The church is a vital, living organism of which Christ is

the life. This spiritual community derives its powers from the head. Christ should govern and direct the life of the whole church and of its individual members, in their business and social affairs and in all personal relationships of life.

Dear Lord, we are grateful for our church and home. May we continually seek thy leadership as supreme head and give thee preeminence in all things. In Jesus' name we pray. Amen.

The People of God
(Read I Peter 2:1–10)

Christians must frequently reexamine their responsibilities as God's people. Self-sufficiency, pride in numbers, buildings, and wealth can hinder God's purposes for any religious denomination that has grown rich in members and money.

The human family, as the basic unit in society, gives structure and unity to all that society is and does. So the redeemed (the church) family must be that kind of basic unit in the kingdom of God. Jesus said, "If a house be divided against itself, that house cannot stand" (Mark 3:25, KJV). Over 270 Protestant denominations now exist. We need to emphasize the *spirit* which binds us in Christian love rather than outward forms and superficial interpretations which divide us in petty differences.

Contemporary Christianity cannot move the world very far toward the Christian ideal of being the family of God until more Christians take seriously their responsibility to reveal God's spirit of love in the home, on the farm, at the shop, in the office, in the legislative hall, on the streets—*everywhere*. What are the chances of a workshop for God in our family, our church, and the world?

Dear God, as you have blessed us, help us now to show forth in praise thy redemptive love and mercy. In the name of Jesus we pray. Amen.

Life Together
(Read 1 Corinthians 1:1–9)

God faithfully calls us to fellowship with his son Jesus Christ—life together with him.

Dietrich Bonhoeffer, a German Christian, was executed by special order of Heinrich Himmler on April 9, 1945, shortly before the concentration camp where he was imprisoned was liberated by the Allied forces. His writings throb with the faith of one who has met Jesus Christ and accepted the ultimate consequence of that encounter. In the dark horrors of a concentration camp, Bonhoeffer wrote his little book *Life Together*. In it he says that Christian fellowship is a gift of God which we cannot call our own. Essentially, this fellowship is God's intention expressed through our lives.

Just as the Christian should not be constantly feeling his spiritual pulse, so too, the Christian community has not been given to us by God for us to be constantly taking its temperature. The more thankfully we daily receive what is given to us, the more surely and steadily will fellowship increase and grow from day to day.[9]

This gift of community is to be shared with others who would become a part of the Christian fellowship. The Christian is to declare to them what God in Christ has done for him, "so that they may fellowship with us."

In Jean-Paul Sartre's starkly realistic play *No Exit*, he strikingly portrays three people in hell, each trapped in a room without exit, unable to communicate with one another their distress, or any emotion or thought. The absence of fellowship, especially in times of distress, makes life a hell.

Are there times in our family when we give one another the silent treatment? Communication usually breaks down long before people stop speaking. It is better to argue than to freeze one another out by silent hostility. If we do not learn to communicate in the family, we probably will be unable to get through to people outside the family.

Our Father, we thank thee for the fellowship of Christians. Help us to value it more and to share it generously. In the name of Jesus Christ who loved and gave himself for us, we ask it. Amen.

Chosen by Christ
(Read John 15:12–17)

We are thrilled to hear of the "fruits brought forth," as people learn of Jesus through our missionaries. We feel that God has chosen them in some special way to do his work. And indeed he has. Missionaries are appointed to specific places of service to "bring forth fruit" by sharing God's limitless love.

Each member of this family can also be a missionary, in our home, in school, on the job, and in our neighborhood. We have opportunities similar to those of the missionaries in foreign countries. To be chosen as God's messenger means personal involvement wherever we are. It means to express in attitudes and acts the spirit of Christ *today*, with friends, employer or employees, teachers, and certainly with our family.

What amazing, unshakable trust Christ has in ordinary people! Even though we falter and fail, he continues to trust us. Knowing all there is to know about us, he chooses us for fellowship and service in his name.

In Christ, we have a friend to whom we can speak frankly and freely. Everything that touches our lives is of interest to him. In Christ's name we are assured that God will come to us in times of stress. He will open doors which will not yield to mere human strength and wisdom. By asking, in Christ's name, we will find help to live life as God wants it done.

Our Father, make us worthy of thy love. We pray in Jesus' name. Amen.

Growing in Christlikeness
(Read Ephesians 4:4–16)

The greatest achievement for any family is Christian growth. A detailed study of the lives of delinquent boys and girls would help us understand in some measure how character is formed. Some kind of flashback would reveal the importance of the day-to-day choices that a child makes. Parental choices that are related to the child would take on new significance. By a series of choices, good or bad character develops. Parents are a child's first teachers.

David Roberts tells the story of a medieval blacksmith who took immense pride in his work and put a special mark upon everything he made. When a hostile army took over the town, the blacksmith was imprisoned and bound with heavy chains. But he was a powerful man and felt confident that he could break the chains that shackled him. Surely he would find a weak link which he could break and thus gain his liberty. But as he examined the chain, link by link, he found on each the secret mark of his own workmanship. His heart sank in despair because he knew there was not one weak link in the chain.

All our accumulated experiences and the choices we make throughout our lives are like the links of a chain. They finally determine the kind of persons we are—strong or weak, good or bad.

We need the admonition of verses 14 and 15 of today's Scripture passage.

Dear God, help us as a family to grow in Christlikeness. We ask in Jesus' name. Amen.

The Nature of Fellowship
(Read Acts 2:41–47)

An ancient story tells of a man who died and went first to hell and then to heaven. In both places, the inhabitants were just as they had been on earth, except that their elbows would not bend one inch. He could not tell any difference between heaven and hell until he saw the inhabitants of each place seated at the table trying to eat. Here the dramatic difference appeared. In hell, the stiff-elbowed people were in turmoil, knocking one another over the head and unable to eat as each one tried to feed himself.

In heaven, great joy and communion was everywhere because each person with stiff elbows fed the person across the table from him and vice versa! The capacity for interdependence often makes the difference between heaven and hell. It makes the difference between happy, united families and anxious, fragmented ones.

In today's Scripture passage, we see the early Christian family daily "attending the temple together and breaking bread in their homes . . . praising God and having favor with all the people. And the Lord added to their number day by day those who were being saved."

When we are committed to Christ and to one another, our home and church fellowship will be blessed and we will know abundant, meaningful lives as individuals.

Oh God, we pray in Jesus' name specifically for the fellowship of our home and our church and we give thee the praise. Amen.

THE FAMILY'S RELATION
TO OTHERS

Family Schizophrenia
(Read Ephesians 5:21–25)

Many people complain that they do not have
time for each other any more that the business of living—
home duties, work, church, and civic activities—come
between them. They keep burdensome schedules. They
run from daylight to dark. They belong to *everything!*
and are so engrossed in keeping up with buzzers, phones,
the calendar, and the neighbors that they have forgotten
where they came from and are afraid to look where they
are going.

In the far country of twentieth-century living, such a

one, like the prodigal son, had to "come to himself." He returned to his rightful place through a rediscovery of the meaning of the marriage relationship as he examined afresh these biblical affirmations:

Since we are made in the image of God, there is more to each of us than the other sees. The loss of reverence for what each of us is meant to be destroys us and our relationships.

We find our life by giving ourselves and cherishing the other person. Our business is to live so that we can help to strengthen and sustain our partners.

Compatibility is the achievement of marriage, not a condition necessary to its beginning. The Christian doctrine of man teaches that we are not only self-centered but selfish as well. We must work at being compatible in marriage.

It takes time to be married. Taking time to be married is one way a man and woman find a wholeness which is not unrelated to holiness.

Although marriage is a human institution, it is also a gift of grace—and the love which creates lasting happiness comes ultimately from the source of all love—God himself.

O God, help us to have time for one another and for thee. In Jesus' name we pray. Amen.

Hospitality, the Way of Love
(Read I Peter 4:7–11)

The wife of a hard-to-please husband was determined to please him for just one day. "Darling," she asked, "what would you like to eat this morning?" "Coffee and toast, grits and sausage, and two eggs—one scrambled and one fried," he replied. When breakfast was on the table, she stood aside, waiting for a word of praise. After a quick glance, he said, "Well, if you didn't scramble the wrong egg!"

Many times the members of our families need to remember the admonition: "Practice hospitality ungrudgingly to one another." The Scottish preacher, Ian Mc-Laren, said, "Be kind, for nearly everyone you meet is fighting a hard battle."

Hospitality is not an inherent characteristic of man. It is a cultivated virtue which requires specific and persistent effort. In the modern home, bills, little children, fatigue, illness, meetings, job, housework—the list could go on and on—all are realities that try our patience and test our hospitality. An unknown author points out that many times we express our hospitality or inhospitality in one simple word:

A careless word may kindle strife;
A cruel word may wreck a life;
A bitter word may hate instill;
A brutal word may smite and kill;
A gracious word may smooth the way;
A joyous word may light the day;

A timely word may lessen stress;
A loving word may heal and bless.

Dear Lord, help us to see hospitality as a way of love and life in our homes, in our church, and in our community. We pray in Jesus' name. Amen.

"Be Ye Kind"
(Read Ephesians 4:20–32)

Writing to the Christians at Ephesus, Paul tells them that, because they know Christ, they are to put off the old corrupt nature and put on a new nature. They must do away with the old models of pagan behavior because their new natures require a different pattern—Christlikeness.

(Have someone read from a modern translation like J. B. Phillips' *The New Testament in Modern English*, if possible. Let each person recall some of the differences between the old nature and the new nature which Paul mentions. Suggest ways each person can apply this teaching in his life every day. Include ideas about Christian speech, honest work, anger, pride, kindness, forgiveness, and love. Close by repeating together the verse "Be kind one to another, tenderhearted, forgiving one another, as God in Christ forgave you.")

This is one of the first verses we learn as a child, and it stands us in good stead all through life.

Our Father, may we learn to forgive others because of thy great sacrifice for us. Help us to see that thou hast forgiven us so many times and that we must learn to be forgiving in our relationship to others, especially to one another in our family. We pray in Jesus' name. Amen.

Love Thy Neighbor
(Read James 2:1–10)

At the bottom of the Statue of Liberty in New York harbor on an engraved tablet in the star-shaped base are the words:

> Give me your tired, your poor,
> Your huddled masses yearning to breathe free,
> The wretched refuse of your teeming shore.
> Send these, the homeless, the tempest-tost to me,
> I lift my lamp beside the golden door!

The Statue of Liberty continues to be a symbol of hope to the world's needy and downtrodden and a reminder of the American tradition: help for the oppressed and concern for others.

We Christians fulfil the law as we love our neighbor.

In doing this, we experience the joy that is to be found in following Christ. A man gains a more adequate appreciation and understanding of himself when he projects his love for his neighbor.

(Talk about some specific ways in which each family member can show Christian concern for others. Ask, who is our neighbor?)

Help us, our Father to fulfil the royal law by loving others in a meaningful way through Jesus Christ our Lord. Amen.

Things Which Make for Peace
(Read Romans 14:13–23)

A wife told her minister how she and her husband irritated each other and lost their patience with each other at the least provocation.

"What you need in your home is a menagerie," the minister said.

"Well, we have a cat and a dog and a canary," she answered not understanding at all what he meant.

"No," he said, "what you need is two bears." When she looked even more puzzled, he added, "And their names are bear and forbear."

The six most difficult words to utter are "I was wrong; I am sorry." Yet these words are so needed in our families.

They are among the "things which make for peace."

Patient love expresses itself in a willingness on the part of each to accept the other for what he is. One grievous danger in any marriage is the reforming urge. Marriage is no reform school. We resent being made over, and anyone who tries to make over another person is in for a rough time. Promises made during courtship can be short lived unless an effort to keep them is made repeatedly.

(Take a few moments to talk about specific things which make for peace in your home, in your church, among friends, or where you work. How can you help one another?)

Dear God, lead us to follow after the things which make for peace in all our relationships. Help us to support and encourage one another in the spirit of Jesus. Amen.

Father Forgives
(Read Colossians 3:12–17)

One summer afternoon a small boy was riding home on his bicycle from the park where he had been swimming. A speeding automobile hit him. He was rushed to the hospital, and his family was notified of his serious injury. With their pastor, the parents waited outside the emergency room. Several minutes elapsed. Then a doctor emerged and announced that the boy had died. The father and mother stood trembling like leaves in a storm. Their tragic loss seemed more than they could bear.

During the trial of the man whose automobile had hit the boy, a dramatic court scene occurred. The boy's father walked across the room to the man, extended his hand and said, "I want you to know that I do not hate you, that I have forgiven you." The headline of the paper the next day was "Father Forgives Man Who Killed Son."

Do you remember what Jesus said as he hung on the cross? "Father, forgive them; for they know not what they do." How much like our Saviour was this earthly father. In the midst of his deep sorrow, he did not lose contact with God. Through Christ, he was able to forgive one who had brought him heartache.

(Close with a few minutes of silent meditation—asking for personal forgiveness and the grace to forgive others. Have one member close with prayer.)

Accept our prayers, in the name of Jesus who paid the supreme price for our forgiveness. Amen.

Brotherly love
(Read Romans 12:9–21)

Our Scripture passage has special meaning for us today. We need to heed Paul's admonition in verses 9-10 especially.

Four-fifths of the people of the world are hungry, and "out of the 2200 million people in the world, 1700 million, usually in debt all their lives, are in want, more or less oppressed and exploited, and increasingly unhappy and determined to be free from want."[10] Yet in America 480 million dollars are spent annually just to store our surplus grain and food, while 100,000 persons a day die of starvation. The National Study Conference on the Church and Economic Life has said, "The hunger of any man anywhere becomes the concern of Christian men everywhere."

Christians in every century have to learn to "be kindly affectioned one to another." Perhaps there is no place where this kind of commitment is more needed than in our homes. It seems easier to give time, kindness, and appreciation to others than to members of our family. Our wives, husbands, brothers, sisters, or parents often receive only what is left over of our emotions. We need the support of each person's affection, patience, understanding, and acceptance. Christians need to have this same kind of relationship within their church family. Do we hold unwarranted prejudices about our brothers? Do we always act in brotherly love?

(Suggest closing the family worship period with

sentence prayers in which each one asks for help to live peaceably with all men and to overcome evil with good.)

Undergird with Prayer
(Read I Timothy 2:1–8)

In London Billy Graham asked: "Queen Elizabeth, how do you summarize the world situation?" "Terrifying!" was her terse reply. That world powers have enough atomic weapons to destroy the people of the world *is* terrifying.

On the basis of man's past performance, some people say that war is inevitable. Others say it is unthinkable in the atomic age. What can we do? *Our* fingers are not on the trigger.

The roots of most wars lie in personal hostility. Modern psychology would confirm James' words: "What causes wars, and what causes fightings among you? Is it not your passions that are at war in your members?" (James 4:1). Every person is part of the problem or part of the solution. Today's Scripture passage confronts the Christian with an ethical idealism.

Paul exhorted us to pray for all men. He considered prayer a matter of primary importance. Although many people recognize the personal benefits resulting from prayer, they find it difficult to pray for all men and to believe that prayer has meaning beyond the personal life of the one who prays. Yet, prayer is enjoined for "kings, and for all that are in authority."

Confronted by world chaos, the Christian can further the cause of world peace by achieving peaceful relationships in his personal life and by undergirding with prayer the efforts of those who work for peace at high political levels—local, national, and international.

(Mention by name any member of your family, a close friend, or a member of your church holding a public office and resolve to support him [or her] frequently in prayer.)

O God, help us to understand thy purposes as we pray for all men that thy peace may rule in our hearts and our homes. We pray in the name of Jesus our Lord. Amen.

Itching Ears
(Read 2 Timothy 4:1–8)

Paul warned Timothy that some people will not endure sound teachings but will seek teachers who simply agree with their own thinking.

Always some men want to hear only pleasant things. They applaud men who "pat them on the back" and exalt teachers who say the things they want to hear.

We can recall sermons in which the minister reaffirmed

our views about certain things. We responded enthusiastically and declared the sermon to be one of the greatest ever heard. Students criticize a teacher with whom they disagree, even though his teaching is sound and correct. They may have developed "itching ears" and would accept only a teacher who would "scratch" them!

Paul warned Timothy that he must be prepared to be forsaken by people who insisted on having teachers who would "rubber stamp" their own opinions. But, "as a good soldier, Timothy was to remain steady, to preach the gospel."

Children sometimes scorn the sound teaching of their elders. Some differences of opinion naturally exist between the generations. But young people need to heed the counsel of older persons who would share the truth and wisdom they have accumulated through the years.

Our Father, help us to accept thy truth revealed through thy Word in Jesus Christ. Amen.

Answers in the Back
(Read Ephesians 2:13–22)

In an effort to show how Christ is the answer Paul has pointed out in these Scriptures the way of reconciliation. Strangers no more! We have been reconciled "unto God in one body by the cross."

This is the message that I bring,
A message angels fain would sing:
"Oh, be ye reconciled,"
Thus saith my Lord and King,
"Oh, be ye reconciled to God."

E. TAYLOR CASSEL

While Dr. W. A. Welsh was pastor of the East Dallas Christian Church, he referred to the slogan, "Christ is the Answer," and asked, "Is it as simple as that?" He recalled that in college he had thought of majoring in mathematics. When he came to solid geometry, he found that his brain was more solid than the geometry book. So he decided to change courses. His roommate said, "Here's a snap course, trigonometry! All the problems are in the front of the book; all the answers are in the back."

Welsh thought this was fine, and he registered for trigonometry. But there was more to it than just outlining the problems in the front of the book and finding the answers in the back. Between these two stages, the professor expected the student to work out certain complicated equations whereby, given a particular problem, they could demonstrate how they arrived at the answer.

In the personal equations of family problems we must prove to unbelievers how we arrived at the answer which we have found in Christ. To say that he is the answer is not enough; we must demonstrate in our family and in other relationships how we came to this conclusion.

(Talk about the meaning of this reconciliation in the household of God and in our families.)

Dear God, we thank thee that in mercy you forgive us,

in love you claim us, and in grace you redeem and reconcile us. Help every member of our family to be mindful of these gifts and to know that Christ is indeed the answer. We pray in his name. Amen.

THE FAMILY AND THE COMPASSIONATE SAVIOUR

Salvation Has Come to This House
(Read Luke 19:1–10)

Zacchaeus was a despised tax collector for the Roman government. Probably, he had robbed the poor, cheated the ignorant, and used every underhanded method he knew to increase his profits. Why did he want to see Jesus? Was his conscience causing him grief? Maybe he had heard that Jesus received sinners and ate with them. Whatever had been his motive, he was so determined to see Jesus that he forgot himself and climbed a sycamore tree.

When Jesus called Zacchaeus to come down, he responded quickly and took Jesus to his house. Later he confessed his sins, and Jesus said, "Today salvation has come to this house." A great thing happened in Zacchaeus' house that day. He found Jesus in his own home.

Jesus is always seeking the lost, the lonely, the anxious, the downhearted. They may be found in every crowd, in every neighborhood, in every apartment building, in every housing project. They are the unseen ones. They often seem unfriendly, unneighborly, "stuck up," aloof.

"What's the matter with them?" we ask. "Why don't they speak?"

In all probability, they are not conceited but lonely. Perhaps they are waiting, as was Zacchaeus, for someone to "invite them."

We have offended against thy holy laws, O God, and we are like lost sheep. But we thank thee that thou didst come into our houses to seek and to save the lost. We would receive thy love and forgiveness this day. In Jesus name we pray. Amen.

Father, into Thy Hands
(Read Luke 23:39–49)

One man, inflicted by blindness, becomes a whining beggar with a tin cup. Another blind man,

John Milton, produced *Paradise Lost* and *Paradise Regained.*

One man, struck down by polio becomes a whimpering, complaining cripple. Another polio victim, Franklin Delano Roosevelt, became president of the United States.

One man, on a cross, scoffed and scorned in bitter revilement. Jesus Christ, nailed to a cross, committed his life to God: "Father, into thy hands I commit my spirit!"

All of us have to face conflict with sin, temptation, physical or emotional difficulties and, finally, death itself. But the way in which we face these things is a testimony, for or against, to the faith we live by. These are vital stages of the growth process.

(Give opportunity for the members of the family to share examples of persons they have known who have made stepping-stones out of stumbling blocks by committing their lives to the Father.)

Father, not only in death but also in life do we commit ourselves to thee for safekeeping through Jesus Christ our Saviour. Amen.

Ask . . . Seek . . . Knock
(Read Luke 11:1–13)

This Scripture passage is concerned with the reality of faith in our daily lives.

Faith is a present and sustaining motive for action. It is trust that finds expression in action based on our belief. The Christian's faith is characterized by the continuing response of the whole man to God as revealed in Jesus Christ. The Christian commits to Jesus Christ his mind and heart, his obedience and destiny, his very self.

Such faith is marked by expectancy. We come to God believing that "he is, and that he is a rewarder of them that diligently seek him." Our prayers are often dreary and meaningless because we expect nothing to happen. Church worship is sometimes dull and unsatisfying because people expect nothing from the service. In our families we can take one another for granted and degenerate into a domestic highway where we pass one another on the way to our next appointment.

When "nothing happens" and no special awareness of God's presence or blessing is experienced in our church and families, it usually is related to a problem of faith—"according to your faith be it unto you."

Dear Father God, we ask because thou hast said to ask. Help our family and our church to find clear meaning for existence. We seek and knock in the confident faith that thy will may be opened unto us. In Jesus' name we pray. Amen.

Dark Gethsemane
(Read Luke 2:39-53)

It was the habit of Margaret Fuller to exclaim, in her eager, happy, heroic manner, "I accept the universe." When this was told to Carlyle, the old man remarked sardonically, "She'd better!"

William James uses the story to emphasize the importance which acceptance of the universe has on morality and religion. He asks these questions: "Do we accept it only in part and grudgingly, or heartily and altogether? Shall our protests against certain things in it be real, radical, and unforgiving; or shall we think that, even with evil, there are ways of living that must lead to good? If we accept the whole, shall we do so as if stunned into submission, as Carlyle would have us—or shall we do so with enthusiastic assent?" Three ways, three attitudes are open to us, and the joy of life depends on which one we take—rebellion, resignation, or reconciliation.[11]

In dark Gethsemane Jesus accepted the universe and reconciled it unto himself.

(Have members of the family cite biblical examples of persons who viewed life with rebellion—Adam and Jonah, with resignation—Elijah and Job, and with reconciliation—Jesus and Paul. Point out that times have changed, but the same attitudes appear in every generation.)

Father, as we pass through our personal, dark Gethsemanes, give us the courage to pray, not our wills but thine be done. In Jesus' name. Amen.

The Meaning of Salvation
(Read Acts 2:23–31)

Ask the family members, What does salvation mean? Give each member a chance to respond.

Salvation means two things: *rescue,* as when a lifeguard saves a person from drowning, and *to put in a safe place,* as when a boy saves a dollar in his bank.

Christians use this word in both ways. Christ rescues us from sin, death, and Satan, and he puts us in the safety of God's protection. Through Christ we are rescued and safe. We are rescued to live for God, and we are saved from evil to lovingly serve God.

Paul was able to convince some of the Jews in Rome that Jesus was the Messiah, but others would not believe. Paul spoke to them in the words of the prophet Isaiah, verses 26-27.

Paul was a prisoner in Rome, relatively free to go about his way unmolested. How and when he died is not recorded. Perhaps it is better this way, for in one sense Paul never died. He had been rescued by Jesus Christ and put safely into God's eternal care.

O Father, for the privileges of our salvation through Jesus Christ, for the knowledge of him and the meaning of this gift, given to us through the writings of Paul, we thank thee in Jesus' name. Amen.

He Cannot Deny Himself
(Read 2 Timothy 2:8–13)

Young Mary was learning to cook boiled custard. "Stay right there and stir it every minute," her Mother instructed, "and turn the heat down so it won't scorch." In a few minutes the doorbell rang. Mary's friend had just received a record she had ordered. The girls listened intently to the record forgetting the boiling, sticking custard. It scorched!

Several years passed and Mary married. Later, when she had to return home for a week to care for her mother, during a period of illness she prepared boiled custard one afternoon. As the family enjoyed it, they recalled Mary's many failures before she became a fine cook. Mary thanked her mother for never giving up on her while she learned to cook. Holding out a spoon of custard her mother said, "I wouldn't have denied myself the privilege of having such wonderful meals for anything in the world!"

Christians need to remember God's faithfulness. He is constantly at work, through the Spirit of Christ, guiding, teaching, drawing us together in fellowship with him. However often we may sin and fail, the Father waits with unchanging love to redeem our mistakes.

God does not cease to exist when men cease to believe or trust him. He has endowed men with the freedom to reject or accept him. God, however, remains faithful.

Our Father, we are grateful for thy faithfulness to us as a family. Help us to keep our trust firmly in thee. We ask in Jesus' name. Amen.

THE FAMILY AND THE
RISEN SAVIOUR

The Purpose of Easter
(Read Luke 24:36–43)

The body of Abraham Lincoln lay in state in Cleveland. An elderly Negro woman stood in the line holding a little child in her arms. After gazing a long time into the face of the emancipator of her people, the woman whispered to the child, "Take a long, long look, honey. That man died for you."

The Easter Season affords us a long look at Jesus Christ whose victory over death has provided for us an abundant and eternal life.

After Jesus' crucifixion, the disciples were restless and

uneasy. Gone was their high vision to change the world under the leadership of Jesus. With that torn, lifeless body lying there in the tomb, what could they do? Then the risen Lord appeared and said to them, "Why are you troubled, and why do questionings rise in your hearts? See my hands and my feet, that it is I myself; handle me, and see; for a spirit has not flesh and bones as you see that I have."

It was too good to be true, but it was. Their faith was restored, their courage renewed. *Then* they began to change their world. Jesus' resurrection validated every claim he had made. It validates the faith of Christians today. Because Christ won victory over sin on the cross, he conquered death in the grave. His resurrection certified his victory to all men, for all time.

O God, help us to see thy risen son and to change our world because of that vision. Give us, we pray, the direction and leadership of the Holy Spirit, the courage to face conflict, the confidence to make decisions, and the desire to share with others the abundant life we know. We ask this in Jesus' name. Amen.

The Lord Is Risen
(Read Luke 24:28–35)

A little boy, standing beside an eminent preacher as they both viewed Rubens' famous painting *Descent from the Cross,* said, "Mister, that's Jesus. They killed him. They were wicked to kill him, 'cause he was good. They are taking his body down now to bury it." He paused a moment, his face glowing. "But, Mister," he added, "he didn't stay dead—he didn't stay dead!"

The Lord is risen indeed! His resurrection was God's seal of authority on everything that went on from Bethlehem to Calvary. It was the blue pencil mark drawn through everything else that was extraneous to God's purpose. He had edited his story, all scribbled over as it had been, and with his own hand! The truth that God was in Jesus Christ redeeming the world emerged clean and uncluttered. The Lord is risen!

The movement of life is toward the gospel, not away from it. The saving purpose of God is over all the chaos we fashion for ourselves. The pageant is headed in his direction, and we pull it off course at our peril.

(Ask: In what practical ways does belief in the Lord's resurrection make a difference in our family?)

Heavenly Father, grant us eyes to see and hearts to believe that he is risen. Let this belief make a difference in our family this day. We pray in Christ's name. Amen.

Not Just a Number
(Read I Corinthians 15:12–22)

In a world which is increasingly impersonal, we are designated by numbers at both ends of life. A mother today is Maternity Case No. 8434, and her child, after being fingerprinted and footprinted and decorated with an ankle bracelet, becomes No. 8003. At the other end of the pilgrimage, a modern funeral in our great cities becomes an event in Parlor B on a certain day, with preacher No. 14 and singer No. 77, flowers and decoration Class B. In our wallets may be a collection of numbers. Our driver's license has a number; so has our car. We have a Social Security number and an insurance policy number. The state and various stores have numbers for us. We are identified by cards in some vast index.

But Easter affirms that we are not numbers but children of God, with an eternal place in his mind and love. Jesus' resurrection guarantees the reality of resurrection for all believers.

We need not be afraid of any amazement in life, for we have read the "script" through to the end, "Christ Is Risen." It came out all right.

Our Father, we thank thee for the risen Christ, and we know that our faith in him who died and rose again for us is not in vain. Amen.

Feed My Sheep
(Read John 21:15-19)

When Jesus called Peter to follow him, Peter rose up at once, left all, and followed. But later before the crucifixion he completely failed Christ and disloyally denied him three times.

After his resurrection, Jesus asked Peter three times whether he loved him, and three times Peter replied that he did. Each time Peter added, "You know that I love you." Peter faced this hard test without protest or argument. He knew he had shown little evidence of love. He could not forget his desertion. And though he had not yet been able to prove it, he knew that in spite of everything he loved Christ. He confidently called Christ himself as his witness.

What other plea do any of us have? We also have failed Christ too often. As with Peter, he accepts our plea of love if indeed we truly love him.

Three times, Jesus instructed Peter to feed his lambs or sheep. Thus, he restored Peter to his position as a leader and gave him responsibility for the Christian group. Christ bade Peter to do two things for them—tend and shepherd them and feed them.

Christ bids parents and churches alike to tend and nurture those whom God has placed in their care.

Our Father, may our actions this day reveal our love for thee. We pray in Jesus' name. Amen.

Our Marching Orders
(Read Matthew 28:16–20)

One day a minister asked the Duke of Wellington if he thought foreign missions should be carried on. The Iron Duke asked, "What are your orders?" The minister quoted the Great Commission. "What!" exclaimed the Duke. "That is your order and you discuss doing it?" To a man who was trained to obey an order, to debate the matter seemed treason. So it is!

"All nations" are recurring words in Jesus' teaching. The gospel contains a worldwide dimension and imperative. The "go ye" is not an alternative. It is a joyful mandate. We learned of Christ through other Christians, and we must share with thanksgiving the gift we have received. The marching orders remain: "Go ye."

Every Christian may not be called to so-called full-time Christian service, but every Christian has been called of God to full-time Christian living and witnessing. In this sense, every Christian is called to a missionary ministry.

A young nurse expressed this concept beautifully when she said, "Some day, God may lead me to Africa or Japan. If he does, I will go gladly. Now, however, the patients to whom I minister in the Baptist hospital are my mission field, and I want my witness to be the best I can give."

Wherever we may be, we are entrusted with the privilege of sharing the salvation that brings men into a relationship with God that results in new life and joy.

Dear God, help each member of our family to take

seriously the marching orders given by thy Son Jesus, in whose name we pray. Amen.

Entrusted with a Commission
(Read I Corinthians 9:15–22)

The steamship *Californian* passed only ten miles from the sinking *Titanic*, but a friend of its wireless operator was playing with the set and no messages were heard. Fifteen hundred and seventeen lives were lost when the "unsinkable" steamer struck an iceberg at 11:40 P.M., April 15, 1912.

The S.S. *Carpathia* was a far greater distance from the sinking *Titanic* than was the *Californian*. But no one in the wireless room was "playing with the set." The cries of distress were heard, and the S.S. *Carpathia* arrived in time to save several hundred lives. The *Californian*, only ten miles away, became aware of the tragic loss only after it was too late.

Every Christian is responsible for evangelizing, teaching, and training the people in his community as well as being responsible for people in other lands. The task is urgent, and it must begin at home.

(Ask each member of the family how he may be a witness for Christ this day.)

Dear God, may we not play at missions while a world is being lost. Help us to have the antennas of our souls turned to thee. We pray in Jesus' name. Amen.

Keep on Keeping On
(Read Luke 9:57–62)

The first phonograph invented by Thomas Edison was unsatisfactory. The high tones were harsh and the low ones muffled. Edison employed a man to perfect the instrument. For two years he worked tirelessly trying to improve it. Discouraged, he went to Edison planning to quit. The great inventor perceived the man's sense of failure and said, "I believe that for every problem God has given us, he has a solution. We may not find it, but someday someone will. Go back and try a while longer."

One factor that contributed to Edison's success as an inventor was his unfaltering determination to remain loyal to a worthy idea. No one ever heard him giving excuses for not attempting something difficult.

In the film, *Madam Curie,* there is a scene between Pierre and Madame Curie. They had worked steadily on a project with radium. After 487 experiments in their laboratory, they still had found no solution. Pierre said, "It can't be done; it can't be done! Maybe in a hundred years it can be done, but never in our lifetime." Madame Curie responded, "If it takes a hundred years, it will be a pity, but I dare not do less than work for it as long as I have life."

Loyalty to Christ demands determination to attempt some things which he leads us to do and to keep trying despite obstacles and failure.

(Ask the family if they are reluctant or fearful about facing something difficult. If a particular situation is shared, ask what the person plans to do about overcoming his uncertainty in going on. Ask if other family members can help in any way.)

God, our Father, help us to follow the leading of thy Holy Spirit. May we be loyal to thee through our difficulties, our decisions, our work, in our school and home. We pray in Jesus' name. Amen.

THE FAMILY'S
TOTAL COMMITMENT

Where Are You Going?
(Read Romans 12:1–8)

A story is told of a wealthy old man who was lost in a forest when he finally met a ranger. "Who are you, and where are you going?" the ranger asked. The questions so impressed the old man that he later hired the ranger to wake him each morning and ask, "Who are you? Where are you going?"

In our age of conformity, we need to ask ourselves who we are and where we are going. The world can squeeze us into its mold and restrain our spiritual progress. Only a renewal of our minds and a commitment to the will of

God can prevent this. "Be transformed by the renewal of your mind, that you may prove what is the will of God, what is good and acceptable and perfect." Every Christian needs to experience a sense of identity and direction. A transformed life through Jesus Christ makes this possible.

(Have one member of the family call each person present by name and ask: "Who are you, and where are you going?" Allow time for individual responses. They will range from confident, precise answers to hesitant, unsure, or doubtful comments. Humorous remarks are often injected by very young children. Use these responses constructively to contribute to the family discussion.)

Close the worship by singing together the first stanza of "Take My Life and Let It Be."

Help us, our Father, to be always in the center of thy will. We pray in Jesus' name. Amen.

Saving Life By Losing Life
(Read Luke 9:18–25)

How is it possible for a person who seeks to save his life to lose it? How can one save his life by losing it?

Jesus reminds us that if we gather life to ourselves, we will surely lose it. A story is told of a young fellow who once found a five-dollar bill on a highway. Afterwards, he never lifted his eyes from the ground where he was walking. In forty years he accumulated 29,516 buttons, 54,172 pins, 70 pennies, a bent back, and a miserly disposition. He lost the glories of sunlight and sunset, the smile of friends, the beauty of trees and flowers, and the opportunity to serve his fellowman, and to spread happiness, and to walk with God. We rob life of meaning when we seek security in self-devotion or in some material values.

Only as we lose our life in Christ, do we save it. He sets us free by ruling us. Our greatest need is not for things we can own, but for the One to whom we can belong.

It matters to God what we decide to do with our lives, whether we stand or fall, whether we are disciplined or not. For, in every decision of every day, our future is being determined. It is important for young people to be conscious of this in their school life and date life! Through daily victories, life really changes direction and becomes meaningful.

As we lose our selfish lives to Christ's way of life, we are saved from the enslavement of housekeeping, of job, of keeping up with the Joneses, and of total meaninglessness.

Our God and Father, help us to gain life by daily losing our lives for Christ's sake. We ask in his name. Amen.

It Makes a Difference
(Read Philippians 2:1–11)

A popular saying is: "It makes no difference what you believe just so long as you are sincere." This is not true anywhere. Imagine a chemistry laboratory where there are three bottles on a table: one bears the symbol H_2SO_4 (sulphuric acid); another symbol HCL (hydrochloric acid); and another H_2O (water). To the untrained eye they appear alike; all are liquids and are colorless. A perfectly sincere person, mistaking the sulphuric acid for drinking water, is no less dead than another who drank the powerful acid intentionally. One was sincerely wrong, and both are sincerely dead!

> Poor Willie, he has gone from us;
> His face we'll see no more,
> For what he thought was H_2O
> Was H_2SO_4.

Certain doctrines and beliefs are essential. Belief in Jesus Christ as Lord and Saviour is the foundation of Christian faith and doctrine. This affirmation brings our redeemed lives under the lordship and leadership of Christ. Is Christ truly Lord in our homes among our family members?

At the name of Jesus, O God, we bow and confess that he is Lord of our lives to thy glory. Amen.

On Things Above
(Read Colossians 2:20 to 3:4)

Some clocks have to be wound with a key before they will run. As long as someone remembers to wind the clock, it keeps perfect time. When it fails to get proper attention, it begins to run slowly and eventually stops. The clock then stands motionless until someone helps it to perform the task it was made to do—keep time.

Our lives are somewhat like the clock. We are dependent upon someone outside ourselves to "wind us up" and keep us in good repair for day-to-day living. The One who made us offers the best help. A Christian's life runs more smoothly if his daily life is "oiled" with "those things which are above." Advertizers offer many things for our "run-down conditions," but only God holds the key that keeps our spiritual lives running.

Remedies are not to be found in items we can purchase. People try many things in order to create enthusiasm and vitality—vitamins, pleasure trips, new cars, alcohol, clubs, and various activities. The effect is temporary, and body, mind, and spirit become even more run down. Focusing on material interests to the exclusion of "things above" decreases spiritual vitality—the life in Christ.

Christians are to be hard at work in their world, not withdrawn from it. By seeking spiritual truths from above and thinking on them, by holding fast to the life in Christ, Christians can usually manage to untangle events that baffle so many families. They find light in the dark and meaning in life.

O Father, help us to live close to thee this day. May others see that our thoughts have been on things above. In Jesus name we pray. Amen.

Run with Patience
(Read Hebrews 11:39 to 12:3)

George Washington Carver, the famous Negro scientist, left this testimony: "I took a peanut and I put it out in my hand and said, 'Mr. Creator, what's in that peanut?' And the Creator said to me, 'You've got brains; you go and find out.'" And that is what he did.

The remarkable discoveries of this great man were the result of a happy alliance of faith and patient perseverance. Dr. Carver was a devout man of childlike faith, who believed that every discovery was a revelation. Moreover, he was a man who toiled unceasingly in his laboratory. This combination of faith and perseverance made him a blessing to mankind.

Across the years we have known many people who kept persevering in faith: a leather-faced farmer who lived with the dignity of a king; a Negro caddy whose inner wealth was in his breadth of heart and visionary mind; a pressured businessman who achieved an inner peace which tension could not destroy; a young widow who, in faith, kept on rearing her children; a ten-year-old boy who, by his Christian commitment, encouraged an entire scout troup despite severe physical handicap.

A man usually turns to God in love and faith or out of despair and anguish, seldom for rational reasons.

However, reason increases understanding and strengthens the foundations of faith. Faith in God demands decision, perseverance, and commitment.

Help us, O God, to realize that as we follow thee in faith, we are in a great company of witnesses. In the name of Jesus we pray. Amen.

One Supreme Purpose

(Read Philippians 3:7–14)

For good or ill, our purposes are developed first in the home. Parents may ask their children, "What is your purpose in life?" Responses vary: To attain happiness; to live a free life; to be popular; to make money; to live my life through music; to serve others. Older children may answer that they are still searching for a purpose in life.

For the apostle Paul, life was inwardly renewed, and given purposeful meaning through Christ.

People with certain advantages—wealth, position, or

popularity—are often criticized. Paul had enjoyed some of these attainments but, as a Christian, he cheerfully regarded them as "loss for the sake of Christ." Paul had found new values and looked through new eyes on everything this world could give him. His supreme purpose was to know Christ in "the power of his resurrection, and . . . share his sufferings, becoming like him in his death."

To know Christ is to love and serve him, to identify our lives with his. Christ brings our lives under new management, and each one finds his own unique fulfilment.

Our Father, may our purpose be to live a new and abundant life in Christ—first in our families, then to the uttermost parts of the earth. Amen.

The Great Commission
(Read Matthew 28:16–20)

The vast increase in world population has created a new and urgent necessity for missions. A recent study shows the world currently adding 45 to 55 million people a year.

By the end of this century, there will be more people in China and India together than are *now living* in the entire world.

All Christian gains will be offset by this booming population growth. Missionaries are urging Christians to take a realistic look at these figures. They challenge the sincerity of every Christian who speaks of "winning the world to Christ." Are we a vital part of the mission movement, at home and abroad, to win the people of the world to Christ?

"Why not leave them alone?"
This question was directed to a missionary by a man who sat next to him on an airplane. They were flying over Djakarta, an Indonesian city of approximately four million inhabitants. The man was referring to non-Christian peoples. "After all," he continued, "they have their own way of life. Why come around the world to change it? Wouldn't they *really* be better off if you just left them alone?" . . .

"Leave them alone?" pondered the missionary as the airplane drew near Singapore. "Even if Christians stay at home, *these people will not be left alone.*" He described to his companion the awesome "missionary" work being done by communism. The disciples of Karl Marx have not looked at the world's masses and said, "Leave them alone." They are desperately earnest about changing all men to their sinister pattern, and no response could be more tragic than that of a lazy, cold, indifferent Christianity.[12]

Dear God, help each member of our family to take seriously the Great Commission given by thy Son Jesus, in whose name we pray. Amen.

One Thing Lacking
(Read Luke 18:18–30)

For three weeks the crew of the U.S.S. *Ticonderoga* prepared it for combat. On July 1, 1945, the ship steamed out of Leyte Gulf to join the task force operating off the Japanese mainland. After two days out, a change in orders was made. A cog was missing in the number two reduction gear. Instead of joining the task force, the ship had to make a three-day trip to Guam to repair the gear. One cog had hindered the entire mechanism of the Navy's largest aircraft carrier.

A young man came to Jesus seeking eternal life. From all outward appearances, his life was in perfect condition. By the standards of men there was no criticism of him. He was an upright, moral man. But Jesus discovered that one cog—the willingness to forego all else to follow him—was missing in the mechanism of his life.

Jesus demands complete allegiance and commitment of our time, talent, and money. This must become the Christian's way of life and thus a way to eternal life. Unless Christ controls our riches and possessions, they eventually will control us.

O Lord, help us to examine our hearts this day and whatever is lacking, whatever is keeping us from commitment to thee, fill this vacuum with thy divine love. We ask in Jesus' name. Amen.

Dodging Responsibility
(Read Acts 24:22–27

Felix never rendered a decision in Paul's case. He was alarmed by the truth Paul spoke. He hoped Paul would pay him money, and for two years he kept him a prisoner. Felix, like many public officials, was in a dilemma. He had certain good, basic values that had never been completely smothered. On the other hand, he lived and worked in a world where such values had little chance against selfish enterprise. Caught between the truth of a man's innocence and his desire for public prestige, he dodged his responsibility. But he was finally undone and recalled to Rome for mismanagement of the government. "How are the mighty fallen!" And how great his memorial might have been!

Too often, Christians offer flimsy excuses to avoid responsibility. Some of them are unbelievable: "It's too hot in the summer and too cold in the winter to go to church any more." "I can't make it. You see, my house is too close to the church to get my car out, and it's just a little too far to walk."

But God is no more pleased with our excuses today than he was in times past.

O Lord, help us not put off living for thee in our family and church. In Jesus' name we pray. Amen.

For Me to Live
(Read Philippians 1:12-21)

Five-year-old Eddie was told that his beloved father had been killed. Christian hope and faith surely must have been real in his home. For Eddie took his father's Bible to the funeral home, placed it in the casket, and said, "I know Daddy will want his Bible in heaven." Eddie had been taught the hope and faith of which Paul spoke.

Many people look at life through glasses of hopelessness. They see only disappointment and defeat, having lost the true and noble purpose of life. For them the future is blurred.

All of us need the hope which Christ offers. None of us is sufficiently wise or strong enough to go from the basket to the casket without hope. It does not matter how much wealth, wisdom, or authority we may gain. There are times when these are useless in guiding us safely through the storms of life.

O God, we know that faith, hope, and love are the supreme values in all that has to do with our lives. Help us to live these three timeless virtues in our home and community. In Christ's name we pray. Amen.

Part III Addendum

HOME DEDICATION

(A service which may be used in the inauguration of daily family worship, or when occupying a new home. It can also be used repeatedly in the Christian home. The leader may be father, mother, pastor, or any member of the household.)

Because we are grateful to God for giving us new life in Christ,
Because our life together in the home is blessed by his presence,
Because he alone is deserving of our worship . . .
We pledge ourselves to read the Bible and pray together daily in our home.

The Dedicatory Prayer—Leader
  "Blest Be the Tie"—Sung by family
  Scripture: Psalm 127 (or Col. 3:12–21)

The Lord's Prayer—Offered in unison by family

Repeat responsively—

Leader: To Thee, O God, from whom cometh every good and perfect gift;

Family: We dedicate our home.

Leader: To the fulfilment of our spiritual responsibilities one toward another;

Family: We dedicate our home.

Leader: To Christian character building through patient discipline, understanding guidance, and prayerful counsel;

Family: We dedicate our home.

Leader: To Christian conversation, good reading, and other wholesome activities;

Family: We dedicate our home.

Leader: To choice companions, helpful hospitality, a worthy social life;

Family: We dedicate our home.

Leader: To personal and family worship through Bible reading and prayer;

Family: We dedicate our home.

Leader: To the service of Christ through his church;

Family: We dedicate our home.

Leader: To the glory of Jesus Christ our Saviour and Lord, whose presence we shall ever welcome, the unseen guest at every table, and the silent listener to every conversation;

Family: We dedicate our home.

—————————————   (signed)—————————————
          date
                               (signed)—————————————

"For where two or three are gathered together in my name, there am I in the midst of them" (*Matt.* 18:20).[13]

NOTES

1. *The Hope of a New World* (New York: Macmillian Co., 1942), p. 30.

2. "Granite, Gray Matter, and Grace," *Pulpit Digest,* July, 1954, p. 16.

3. *An Adventure in Love* (Richmond: John Knox Press, 1956), p. 136.

4. *Guideposts to Creative Family Worship* (New York and Nashville: Abingdon Press, 1953), pp. 43–44.

5. Mazelle Wildes Thomas, *The Family Worships Together* (Boston: The Pilgrim Press, 1949), p. 27.

6. From *The New Testament in Modern English,* © J. B. Phillips, 1958. Used with permission of The Macmillan Company.

7. Hazen G. Werner, *Christian Family Living,* ed. Henry M. Bullock (Nashville: The Graded Press [Now Abingdon Press], 1958), p. 121.

8. Grace Noll Crowell, *Light of the Years* (New York: Harper and Bros., 1936), p. 41.

9. (New York: Harper & Row, 1954), p. 30.

10. Frank Laubach, *Wake Up or Blow Up!* (Westwood, N.J.: Fleming H. Revell Company, 1951), pp. 29–30.

11. Adapted from Stanley I. Stuber and Thomas C. Clark, *Treasury of the Christian Faith* (New York: Association Press, 1949), pp. 320–21.

12. Ross Coggins, *Missions Today* (Nashville: Convention Press, 1963), pp. 40–41.

13. From Broadman Supplies, Nashville, Tennessee. Used by permission.

MATERIALS SUITABLE FOR FAMILY WORSHIP

The Christian Home, The Graded Press, 201 Eighth Avenue South, Nashville, Tennessee 37202

Hearthstone, Box 179, St. Louis, Missouri 63166 (Christian Church and the American Baptist)

Home Life, 127 Ninth Avenue, North, Nashville, Tennessee 37203 (Southern Baptist)

Pathways to God, Box 2499, Warner Press, Anderson, Indiana 46011 (Church of God)

*Presbyterian Life,*Witherspoon Building, Philadelphia, Pennsylvania 19107 (United Presbyterian, U.S.A.)

Presbyterian Survey, Box 341, Ponce de Leon Avenue, N. E., Atlanta, Georgia 30308 (Presbyterian Church, U.S.)

Songs for the Young Child, by Bill F. Leach, Broadman Press. Paper, $1.95.

Songs for the Young Child, No. 1, 2 7-inch, 33⅓ rpm, recordings. $2.49. Available from Baptist Book Stores.

The Secret Place, American Baptist Board of Education and Publication, Valley Forge, Pennsylvania 19481 (American Baptist and Christians)

The Upper Room, 1908 Grand Avenue, Nashville, Tennessee 37212 (The Upper Room)

RELATED REFERENCES

Cook, Walter L. *Meeting the Test: A Book of Devotions for Young People*. New York and Nashville: Abingdon Press, 1960.

_____. *Youth Meditations*. New York and Nashville: Abingdon Press, 1970.

Edens, David and Virginia. *Why God Gave Children Parents*. Nashville: Broadman Press, 1966.

Gilmore, J. Herbert, Jr. *Devotions for the Home*. Nashville: Broadman Press, 1971.

Hein, Lucille E. *One Small Circle: A Book of Family Devotions*. New York and Nashville: Abingdon Press, 1962.

Herzel, Catherine. *The Family Worships Together*. Philadelphia: Muhlenberg Press, 1957.

Jahsmann, Allan Hart, and Simon, Martin P. *Little Visits with God: Devotions for Families with Small Children.* St. Louis: Concordia Publishing House, 1957.

——————. *More Little Visits with God: Devotions for Families with Small Children.* St. Louis; Concordia Publishing House, 1961.

May, Edward. *Family Worship Idea.* St. Louis: Concordia Publishing House, 1965.

Mueller, Charles S. *God's Wonderful World of Words: Devotions for Families with Children Ages 9-13.* St. Louis: Concordia Publishing House, 1963.

Priester, Gertrude Ann. *Let's Talk about God: Devotion for Families with Young Children.* Philadelphia: The Westminster Press, 1967.

The Upper Room. Ask for listing of materials for family devotions. 1908 Grand Avenue, Nashville, Tennessee 37212.

Vogel, Lois. *God and Your Family: Devotions for Families with Children Ages 4-9.* St. Louis: Concordia Publishing House, 1963.

BIBLE
VERSE INDEX

OLD TESTAMENT